JUST 10 MINUTES

JUST **10** MINUTES

Love Food ® is an imprint of
Parragon Books Ltd

Parragon
Queen Street House
4 Queen Street
Bath BA1 1HE, UK

Copyright © Parragon Books Ltd 2007

Love Food ® and the accompanying heart
device is a trade mark of Parragon Books Ltd

Design: Terry Jeavons & Company
Photographer: Mike Cooper
Home economist: Lincoln Jefferson

ISBN 978-1-4075-4909-5

Printed in China

This book uses metric and imperial
measurements. Follow the same units of
measurement throughout; do not mix metric
and imperial. All spoon measurements are
level, unless otherwise stated: teaspoons
are assumed to be 5ml, and tablespoons
are assumed to be 15ml. Unless otherwise
stated, milk is assumed to be full fat, eggs
and individual fruits such as bananas are
medium, and pepper is freshly ground
black pepper.

Recipes using raw or very lightly cooked eggs
should be avoided by children, the elderly,
pregnant women, convalescents, and anyone
suffering from an illness. Pregnant and
breast-feeding women are advised to avoid
eating peanuts and peanut products.

Contents

Introduction 6

1 Meat 8

2 Poultry 32

3 Seafood 54

4 Egg & Cheese 84

5 Vegetarian 110

6 Fruit 140

7 Desserts 160

Index 176

Introduction

If you don't have the time or the inclination to spend a lot of time in the kitchen, but enjoy fresh, tasty wholesome food and creative cooking, then these recipes are for you. All the recipes take ten minutes or less to cook, excluding preparation time. They are full of flavour and goodness, but take little time and effort, as the food is prepared and cooked very quickly.

Convenience foods and ready meals are expensive, often boring and usually have a bland or artificial flavour designed to appeal to a mass market. More importantly they are frequently loaded with preservatives. But 'fast' food doesn't have to mean a cocktail of nasty chemicals. You can cook fresh foods quickly with the minimum of fuss but maximum flavour and, of course, you'll know exactly what has gone into them.

The keys to success are using top quality foods; always choose the freshest and best quality produce for optimum flavour, such as free-range eggs, vibrant fruit and vegetables free from blemishes and bruises, fresh herbs, extra virgin olive oil, etc. A well stocked storecupboard and good utensils make cooking much easier. Basic staples should include rice and pasta. Dried pasta will keep longer than fresh and comes in a variety of shapes and sizes, and cooks in minutes. Good seasoning is particularly important when food is cooked for a short time, so a stock of good wine vinegar, honey, spices, herbs and sauces, such as Tabasco and Worcestershire are invaluable to use in recipes to add interest and variety. Canned fish (sardines, anchovies, tuna), tomatoes, sweetcorn and beans are also excellent to keep in the cupboard and you can use these old favourites to add a new imaginative twist to recipes. Cream and yogurt are wonderfully versatile ingredients, perfect for pouring, whipping and spooning, and will add a smooth richness to both sweet and savoury dishes. In the freezer, ready rolled pastry and good quality ice cream are ideal standbys.

The right tools for the job will make all the difference and will also speed up preparation. Non-stick pans, sharp knives, a couple of whisks, a colander, zester, sieve, wooden spoons and spatulas will all reduce time spent in the kitchen. A food processor or blender is also essential.

There's no fiddly preparation in any of these recipes – just simple, tasty food that looks and tastes fabulous. There really is nothing better or more delicious than making your own meals, so try these trouble-free, straightforward recipes and taste the difference.

1 Meat

Prime cuts of meat are best suited to fast
cooking. A shortcut that will save you time
is to freeze meat for about 30 minutes if
possible, when it will easily cut into wafer
thin slices for stir-fries, for example.
Always cut across the grain to help
tenderize the meat. When grilling, turn
the meat only once during cooking for a
juicier result.

Orange & Lemon-coated Crispy Lamb Cutlets

INGREDIENTS

1 garlic clove, crushed

1 tbsp olive oil

2 tbsp finely grated orange zest

2 tbsp finely grated lemon zest

6 lamb cutlets

salt and pepper

orange wedges, to garnish

serves ❷

1 Preheat the grill. Mix the garlic, oil, grated orange and lemon zest and seasoning together in a bowl.

2 Brush the mixture over the lamb cutlets and cook under the grill for 4–5 minutes on each side. Serve, garnished with the orange wedges.

Herbed Lamb Burgers

INGREDIENTS

450 g/1 lb fresh lean lamb mince

75 g/2¾ oz fresh breadcrumbs

1 onion, finely chopped

3 tbsp chopped fresh herbs, such as mint, rosemary or thyme

1 egg

½ tbsp apple juice

1 tbsp sunflower or olive oil

salt and pepper

4 soft white buns, to serve

lettuce and sliced tomato, to garnish

serves ❹

1 Preheat the grill or light the barbecue if using. Mix the mince, breadcrumbs, onion, chopped herbs, egg, apple juice and salt and pepper together in a large bowl.

2 Divide the mixture into 4 burgers and lightly brush with the oil.

3 Grill, fry or barbecue the burgers for 3–4 minutes on each side.

4 Serve the herbed lamb burgers inside soft white buns and garnish with lettuce and sliced tomato.

Teriyaki Steak

INGREDIENTS

four 150 g/5½ oz beef steaks

salt and pepper

2 tbsp vegetable oil

200 g/7 oz beansprouts, trimmed

4 spring onions, trimmed and finely sliced

FOR THE TERIYAKI SAUCE

2 tbsp mirin (Japanese rice wine)

2 tbsp sake or pale dry sherry

4 tbsp dark soy sauce

1 tsp granulated or caster sugar

serves ❹

1 Season the steaks with salt and pepper and set aside.

2 To make the sauce, combine the mirin, sake or sherry, soy sauce and sugar in a bowl, stirring well.

3 Heat 1 tablespoon of oil in a frying pan over a high heat. Add the beansprouts and fry quickly, tossing them in the hot oil for 30 seconds. Remove from the pan and drain on kitchen paper.

4 Add the remaining oil to the pan and when hot add the steaks. Cook for 1–3 minutes on each side, according to how rare you like your meat. Remove from the pan and keep warm.

5 Remove the pan from the heat and add the sauce and spring onions. Return to the heat and simmer for 2 minutes, stirring until the sauce thickens slightly and is glossy.

6 Slice each steak and arrange on a bed of beansprouts. Spoon over the sauce and serve immediately.

Vietnamese Beef Soup

INGREDIENTS

1.2 litres/2 pints good quality beef stock

1 small fresh chilli, chopped

1 cinnamon stick

2 star anise

2 cloves

225 g/8 oz sirloin or fillet steak, cut into thin strips

300 g/10½ oz rice noodles

4 tbsp chopped fresh coriander

lime wedges, to garnish

serves ❷

1 Heat the stock, chilli and spices in a saucepan until boiling, then reduce the heat and simmer for about 5 minutes.

2 Add the beef strips and simmer for a further 2–3 minutes until cooked to your liking.

3 Cook the noodles according to the packet instructions, then drain and place in 2 serving bowls.

4 Pour over the broth and sprinkle with chopped coriander. Garnish with lime wedges and serve.

Stir-fried Beef with Cashew Nuts

INGREDIENTS

2 tbsp sunflower or olive oil

450 g/1 lb rump steak, cut
into thin strips

1 tbsp black peppercorns,
crushed

2 fresh chillies, deseeded
and finely chopped

bunch of spring onions,
trimmed and thinly sliced
or chopped

115 g/4 oz cashew nuts

FOR THE SAUCE

3 tbsp soy sauce

2 tbsp rice wine or dry sherry

1 tbsp dark brown sugar

1 tsp five spice powder

serves ❷

1 Heat the oil in a preheated wok until smoking.
Add the steak strips, crushed peppercorns,
chillies and spring onions and cook for 3–4
minutes, tossing the wok to cook evenly.

2 Mix all the ingredients for the sauce together
in a bowl and pour into the wok. Cook for
3 minutes, tossing the ingredients until
everything is heated through.

3 Add the cashew nuts and toss to combine.
Serve immediately.

Peppered Steaks in Whisky Cream Sauce

INGREDIENTS

3 tbsp black peppercorns, crushed

four x 175 g/6 oz minute steaks

2 tbsp sunflower or olive oil

seasonal vegetables, to serve

FOR THE WHISKY CREAM SAUCE

150 ml/5 fl oz double cream

2 tbsp beef stock

2–3 tbsp malt whisky

serves ❹

1 Press the crushed peppercorns firmly into the steaks to coat.

2 Heat the oil in a frying pan and when hot, place the steaks in the pan and cook for 1 minute on each side.

3 Remove the steaks and keep warm. Pour off the oil from the pan.

4 Mix the cream, stock, whisky and any juices from the steaks together in a bowl and pour into the frying pan. Heat through, stirring, then pour over the steaks. Serve immediately with seasonal vegetables.

Spicy Pork Meatballs

INGREDIENTS

675 g/1 lb 8 oz fresh lean pork mince

1 garlic clove, finely chopped

1 tsp ground ginger

pinch of ground cloves

½ tsp freshly grated nutmeg

½ tsp ground allspice

½ tsp salt

½ tsp black pepper

2 egg yolks

40 g/1½ oz ground almonds

2–3 tbsp sunflower or olive oil

serves ❹

1 Preheat the grill. Mix the pork mince, garlic, spices, salt, pepper, egg yolks and ground almonds together in a large bowl. Form into balls and brush with the oil.

2 Grill the meatballs, turning from time to time for about 8–10 minutes, or until cooked through.

3 Alternatively, heat the oil in a large frying pan and fry the meatballs for about 8–10 minutes, or until cooked through. Serve immediately.

Ginger Pork

INGREDIENTS

2 tbsp sunflower or olive oil

1-cm/½-inch piece fresh root ginger, peeled and grated

1 garlic clove, crushed

2 boneless pork steaks, cut into thin strips

85 g/3 oz shredded white cabbage

4 tbsp cashew nuts

2 tbsp dark soy sauce

1 tbsp dry white wine

1 tsp granulated sugar

1 tsp sesame oil

salt and pepper

serves 2

1 Heat a wok over a high heat and when smoking, add 1 tablespoon of oil, swirling it around the wok.

2 Add the ginger and garlic and cook quickly for 20 seconds. Add the pork and cook for 3–4 minutes, or until just cooked through. Remove the pork, ginger and garlic from the wok and keep warm.

3 Add the remaining oil to the wok and when hot, add the cabbage and cook for 2–3 minutes until tender. Add the cashew nuts and cook for 3 seconds.

4 Return the pork, ginger and garlic to the wok with the soy sauce, wine and sugar. Cook for 1 minute then add the sesame oil and season to taste with salt and pepper.

Sweet & Sour Pork

INGREDIENTS

1 tbsp vegetable oil

350 g/12 oz lean pork, cut
into 5-mm/¼-inch strips

1 large pepper, deseeded
and sliced

4 spring onions, trimmed
and chopped

450 g/1 lb canned pineapple
pieces in juice

2 tbsp cornflour

3 tbsp wine vinegar

juice of 1 lemon

3 tbsp light soy sauce

2 tbsp granulated sugar

salt and pepper

serves 4

1 Heat the oil in a large frying pan, add the
pork strips and cook for 5 minutes, stirring.

2 Add the pepper and spring onions to the pan
and cook for 3 minutes, stirring until they begin
to soften.

3 Drain the pineapple juice into a bowl,
reserving the pineapple pieces, and whisk in
the cornflour, vinegar, lemon juice, soy sauce,
sugar, salt and pepper.

4 Add the mixture to the frying pan and cook
over a medium heat for 1–2 minutes, stirring
until slightly thickened. Add the reserved
pineapple pieces and heat through for 1 minute.
Serve immediately.

Florentine Ham

INGREDIENTS

good handful of fresh baby
spinach leaves

4 slices ham

salt and pepper

4 eggs

4 tbsp double cream

55 g/2 oz grated cheese, such
as Gruyère or Cheddar

serves ❷

1 Preheat the grill. Put the spinach in a large bowl and pour boiling water over it. Leave to stand until the leaves are wilted, then drain well on kitchen paper.

2 Line 2 small ovenproof dishes with the ham, it doesn't matter if the slices overlap the edges, and spread the spinach evenly over the top. Season well with salt and pepper.

3 Break in the eggs and drizzle over the cream.

4 Sprinkle with the cheese and grill for 8–10 minutes, or until the eggs are cooked to your liking and the cheese is bubbling.

Venison Steaks in Redcurrant Cream Sauce

INGREDIENTS

25 g/1 oz butter

1 tbsp vegetable oil

four x 225 g/8 oz venison steaks

asparagus spears, to serve

FOR THE REDCURRANT CREAM SAUCE

2 tbsp water

2 tbsp redcurrant jelly

175 ml/6 fl oz double cream or crème fraîche

salt and pepper

serves ❹

1 Heat the butter and oil in a frying pan and when hot add the venison steaks. Cook over a high heat for 3–4 minutes on each side, depending on how rare you like your venison.

2 Remove the venison from the pan and keep warm.

3 To make the sauce, add the water to the frying pan and stir well. Add the redcurrant jelly and cream or crème fraîche and bring to the boil. Season to taste with salt and pepper and spoon over the steaks. Serve immediately with asparagus spears.

2 Poultry

When cooking poultry there are a couple of shortcuts that can help you save time in the kitchen. Use ready-cooked chicken or duck breasts for the recipes and reduce the cooking time accordingly. To speed up the cooking time of raw boneless chicken breasts place them between two pieces of greaseproof paper or clingfilm and flatten them with a rolling pin.

Chicken Satay

INGREDIENTS

4 tbsp smooth peanut butter

100 ml/3½ fl oz soy sauce

4 skinless, boneless chicken breasts, cut into thin strips

TO SERVE

freshly cooked rice of your choice

lemon wedges

serves ❹

1 Preheat the grill. Mix the peanut butter and soy sauce together in a bowl until smooth. Stir in the chicken strips, tossing well to coat in the mixture.

2 Thread the chicken strips onto 4 pre-soaked, wooden skewers and grill for about 5 minutes on each side until cooked through. Serve immediately with rice and garnish with lemon wedges.

Chicken with Creamy Penne

INGREDIENTS

200 g/7 oz fresh penne pasta

salt

1 tbsp olive oil

2 skinless, boneless chicken breasts

4 tbsp dry white wine

115 g/4 oz frozen peas

5 tbsp double cream

4–5 tbsp chopped fresh parsley, for sprinkling

serves ❷

1 Cook the penne in a large saucepan of boiling salted water for about 3–4 minutes, or according to the packet instructions, until tender but still firm to the bite.

2 Meanwhile, heat the oil in a frying pan, add the chicken breasts and cook over a medium heat for about 4 minutes on each side.

3 Pour in the wine and cook over a high heat until it has almost evaporated.

4 Drain the pasta. Add the peas, cream and pasta to the chicken breasts in the frying pan and stir well. Cover and simmer for 2 minutes. Serve immediately sprinkled with chopped parsley.

Stir-fried Coconut Chicken

INGREDIENTS

2 tbsp vegetable oil

4 skinless, boneless chicken breasts, cut into strips

1 lemongrass stalk, finely shredded

115 g/4 oz flaked almonds

400 ml/14 fl oz canned coconut milk

3 tbsp light soy sauce

3 tbsp chopped fresh coriander

2–3 tbsp flaked coconut

serves ❹

1 Heat the oil in a wok and when almost smoking, add the chicken strips and stir-fry for 5 minutes until browned.

2 Add the lemongrass, almonds, coconut milk and soy sauce. Bring to the boil then reduce the heat and simmer for 1 minute.

3 Serve immediately sprinkled with chopped coriander and the flaked coconut.

Fragrant Chicken

INGREDIENTS

1 fresh red chilli, deseeded and finely chopped

3 garlic cloves, finely chopped

4 spring onions, trimmed and finely chopped

1–2-cm/½–¾-inch piece fresh root ginger, peeled and cut into wafer thin slices

1 tsp ground coriander

1 tsp ground cumin

4 tbsp olive oil

4 tbsp pine kernels, lightly crushed

salt and pepper

4 skinless, boneless chicken breasts, cut into thin slices

1 tbsp chopped fresh coriander

serves ❹

1 Combine the chilli, garlic, spring onions, ginger, ground coriander, cumin, 3 tablespoons of oil and the pine kernels in a bowl and season with salt and pepper.

2 Heat the remaining oil in a wok and, when very hot, add the chicken slices. Cook over a high heat for about 4 minutes, or until the chicken is browned on both sides.

3 Add the chilli mixture and cook for 4–5 minutes, or until the chicken is completely cooked.

4 Stir in the fresh coriander and serve immediately.

Chicken Nuggets with Barbecue Sauce

INGREDIENTS

4 tbsp dry breadcrumbs

2 tbsp grated Parmesan cheese

2 tsp chopped fresh thyme, or 1 tsp dried

1 tsp salt

pinch of black pepper

2 skinless, boneless chicken breasts, cut into cubes

115 g/4 oz melted butter

FOR THE BARBECUE SAUCE

55 g/2 oz butter

2 large onions, grated

300 ml/10 fl oz cider or wine vinegar

300 ml/10 fl oz tomato ketchup

175 g/6 oz dark brown sugar

1–2 tsp Worcestershire sauce

salt and pepper

serves ❹

1 Preheat the oven to 200°C/400°F/Gas Mark 6. Combine the breadcrumbs, cheese, thyme, and salt and pepper on a large flat plate or in a polythene food bag.

2 Toss the chicken cubes in the melted butter, then in the crumb mixture. Place on a baking tray and bake in the oven for 10 minutes until crisp.

3 Meanwhile, make the sauce. Heat the butter in a saucepan, add the onions and cook over a low heat until soft but not browned.

4 Add the cider, tomato ketchup, sugar, Worcestershire sauce, and salt and pepper to taste and heat, stirring, until the sugar has dissolved completely. Bring to the boil then reduce the heat and simmer for 5 minutes.

5 Remove the chicken from the oven and serve with the sauce.

Chicken in Marsala Sauce

INGREDIENTS

2 tbsp plain flour

salt and pepper

4 skinless, boneless chicken breasts, sliced lengthways

3 tbsp olive oil

150 ml/5 fl oz Marsala

2 bay leaves

1 tbsp butter

boiled rice, to serve

serves ❹

1 Mix the flour, and salt and pepper together on a large plate or in a polythene food bag. Add the chicken and toss to coat.

2 Heat the oil in a frying pan over a medium heat. Add the chicken and cook for about 4 minutes on both sides until tender. Remove from the pan and keep warm.

3 Skim most of the fat from the pan and pour in the Marsala. Add the bay leaves and boil for 1 minute, stirring well, then add the butter with any juices from the chicken and cook until thickened.

4 Return the chicken to the pan and heat through. Serve immediately with boiled rice.

Turkey Cutlets with Parma Ham & Sage

INGREDIENTS

2 skinless, boneless turkey cutlets

salt and pepper

2 slices Parma ham, halved

4 fresh sage leaves

2 tbsp plain flour

2 tbsp olive oil

1 tbsp butter

TO SERVE

freshly cooked red cabbage strips (optional)

lemon wedges, to serve

serves ❷

1 Slice each turkey cutlet in half horizontally into 2 thinner escalopes.

2 Put each escalope between sheets of clingfilm and pat out thinly without tearing. Season each escalope with salt and pepper.

3 Lay half a slice of ham on each escalope, put a sage leaf on top and secure these with a cocktail stick.

4 Mix the flour, and salt and pepper together on a large plate and dust each escalope with the seasoned flour on both sides.

5 Heat the oil in a large frying pan, add the butter and wait until foaming. Add the escalopes and fry over a high heat for 1½ minutes, sage-side down, then turn them over and fry for a further 30 seconds or so until golden brown and tender. Serve immediately with freshly cooked red cabbage strips, if liked, and lemon wedges.

Duck Breasts with Citrus Glaze

INGREDIENTS

55 g/2 oz light brown sugar, plus extra if needed

finely grated zest and juice of 1 orange

finely grated zest and juice of 1 large lemon

finely grated zest and juice of 1 lime

4 duck breasts, skin on

salt and pepper

2 tbsp olive oil

TO SERVE

sugar snap peas

orange wedges

serves ❹

1 Put the sugar in a small saucepan, add just enough water to cover and heat gently until dissolved.

2 Add the zests and juices and bring to the boil. Reduce the heat and simmer for about 10 minutes until the zest is soft, and the liquid is syrupy. Remove the pan from the heat. Taste and add a little more sugar if necessary.

3 Meanwhile, score the skin of the duck breasts with a sharp knife in a criss-cross pattern and rub with salt and pepper.

4 Heat the oil in a frying pan. Place the duck breasts skin-side up in the pan and cook for 5 minutes on each side until the flesh is just pink. Keep warm.

5 Slice the duck breasts diagonally into 5–6 slices and arrange on warmed plates.

6 Arrange the sugar snap peas and orange wedges on each plate, spoon over the glaze and serve immediately.

Asian Duck & Noodle Salad with Peanut Sauce

INGREDIENTS

2 carrots, peeled

2 celery sticks

1 cucumber

three x 140-g/5-oz duck breasts

350 g/12 oz rice noodles, cooked according to the instructions on the packet, rinsed and drained

FOR THE PEANUT SAUCE

2 garlic cloves, crushed

2 tbsp dark brown sugar

2 tbsp peanut butter

2 tbsp coconut cream

2 tbsp soy sauce

2 tbsp rice vinegar

2 tbsp sesame oil

½ tsp freshly ground black pepper

½ tsp Chinese five-spice powder

½ tsp ground ginger

serves ❸

1 Preheat the grill. Cut the carrots, celery and cucumber into thin strips and set aside.

2 Grill the duck breasts for about 5 minutes on each side until cooked through. Leave to cool.

3 Meanwhile, heat all the ingredients for the sauce in a small saucepan until combined and the sugar has dissolved completely. Stir until smooth.

4 Slice the duck breasts. Divide the noodles among 3 serving bowls. Place the reserved carrots, celery and cucumber on top of the noodles, arrange the duck slices on top and drizzle with the sauce. Serve immediately.

Honeyed Duck Stir-fry

INGREDIENTS

2 tbsp clear honey

4 tbsp soy sauce

4 skinless duck breasts, sliced

1 tbsp olive oil

bunch of spring onions, trimmed and sliced

1 small head Chinese cabbage, finely shredded

salt and pepper

serves ❹

1 Mix the honey and soy sauce together in a large bowl. Add the duck slices and toss to coat in the mixture.

2 Heat the oil in a wok or frying pan. Add the duck strips (reserve the honey mixture) and cook quickly for 2 minutes until browned.

3 Add the spring onions, Chinese cabbage and the reserved honey mixture. Cook for 3–4 minutes until the duck is cooked but still a little pink in the centre.

4 Season with salt and pepper and serve immediately.

3 Seafood

There's nothing tastier than sparklingly fresh fish simply cooked. If you're skinning fish yourself, dip your fingers In salt beforehand to give a better grip and faster results. A tip for coating fish is to mix the ingredients for coating the fish in a polythene food bag, add the fish and shake gently until coated.

Garlic-sizzled Prawns
with Chilli Dipping Sauce

INGREDIENTS

2 tbsp sunflower or olive oil

1–2 garlic cloves, crushed

bunch of spring onions,
trimmed and chopped

350 g/12 oz raw prawns

chopped fresh chives or
coriander, to garnish

FOR THE CHILLI DIPPING SAUCE

2 tbsp treacle or molasses

6 tbsp white wine vinegar

2 tbsp Thai fish sauce or light
soy sauce

2 tbsp water

1 garlic clove, crushed

2 tsp grated fresh root ginger

2 tsp finely chopped deseeded
fresh red chilli

serves ❸ to ❹

1 To make the sauce, heat the treacle, vinegar, fish sauce and water in a small saucepan until boiling. Add the garlic, ginger and chilli and pour into a small serving bowl.

2 Heat the oil in a wok or frying pan and add the garlic and spring onions. Cook over a high heat for 2 minutes then add the prawns, stir-frying them for a further 2–3 minutes.

3 Divide among 4 warmed serving plates, garnish with chives and serve with the chilli dipping sauce.

Wine-steamed Mussels

INGREDIENTS

115 g/4 oz butter

1 shallot, chopped

3 garlic cloves, finely chopped

2 kg/4 lb 8 oz live mussels,
scrubbed and beards removed

225 ml/8 fl oz dry white wine

½ tsp salt

pepper

4 tbsp chopped fresh parsley

serves ❹

1 Melt half the butter in a very large saucepan over a low heat. Add the shallot and garlic and cook for 2 minutes. Add the mussels, wine, salt and a sprinkling of pepper.

2 Cover, bring to the boil, then boil for 3 minutes, shaking the pan from time to time.

3 Remove the mussels from the pan with a slotted spoon and place in individual serving bowls. Discard any mussels which haven't opened or that don't close immediately when lightly tapped with the handle of a knife.

4 Mix the remaining butter with the parsley in a small bowl and stir the mixture into the cooking juices in the pan. Bring to the boil and pour over the mussels. Serve immediately.

Oysters au Gratin

INGREDIENTS

115 g/4 oz pancetta or streaky bacon, diced

25 g/1 oz celery, finely chopped

4 asparagus tips, finely chopped

salt and pepper

6 fresh oysters, shucked

25 g/1 oz firm mozzarella cheese, grated

serves ❷

1 Preheat the grill. Cook the pancetta in a small frying pan for 1–2 minutes until crisp. Add the celery and asparagus and season to taste with salt and pepper.

2 Spoon the pancetta and asparagus mixture over the oysters. Sprinkle over the grated cheese.

3 Cook the oysters under a medium-hot grill for 3–4 minutes, or until the cheese is golden brown and melted. Serve immediately.

Pancetta-wrapped Scallops

INGREDIENTS

16 large fresh scallops

8 slices pancetta, halved

1 tbsp olive oil

juice of 1 lemon

pepper

lemon wedges, to serve

serves ❹

1 Preheat the grill. Wrap each scallop in half a slice of pancetta.

2 Mix the oil, lemon juice and a sprinkling of black pepper together in a bowl.

3 Coat the scallops in the mixture and thread onto metal skewers (4 on each skewer). Discard any leftover lemon juice mixture.

4 Cook the scallops under a medium-hot grill for 4–5 minutes, turning once until cooked. Serve immediately with lemon wedges.

Poached Scallops
with Sweet Dill Dressing

INGREDIENTS

serves 4

12 fresh queen scallops with
their corals

finely grated zest and juice
of 2 limes

150 ml/5 fl oz dry white wine

bunch of spring onions,
trimmed and sliced diagonally

salt and pepper

2 tbsp granulated sugar

55 g/2 oz butter

2 tbsp chopped fresh dill

fresh dill sprigs and lime
slices, to garnish

1 Put the scallops in a shallow dish. Mix the
lime zest, juice, wine, spring onions, salt and
pepper, and sugar together in a bowl. Pour the
mixture over the scallops and turn them to
coat well.

2 Heat the butter in a frying pan. Using a
slotted spoon, remove the scallops from the
lime mixture and add to the pan. Reserve the
lime juice mixture. Fry for 2 minutes on each
side until almost tender.

3 Stir the lime juice mixture and chopped dill
into the pan. Bring to the boil and boil rapidly
for 8 minutes until reduced.

4 Serve immediately, garnished with dill sprigs
and lime slices.

Hot & Sour Prawn Soup

INGREDIENTS

300 g/10½ oz raw peeled prawns

2 tsp vegetable oil

2 fresh red chillies, sliced

1 garlic clove, sliced

about 750 ml/1⅓ pints fish stock

4 thin slices fresh root ginger

2 lemongrass stalks, bruised

5 Thai lime leaves, shredded

2 tsp palm sugar or brown sugar

1 tbsp chilli oil

handful of fresh coriander leaves

dash of lime juice

serves ❷

1 Dry fry the prawns in a frying pan or wok until they turn pink. Remove and set aside.

2 Heat the vegetable oil in the same pan, add the chillies and garlic and cook for 30 seconds.

3 Add the stock, ginger, lemongrass, Thai lime leaves and sugar and simmer for 4 minutes. Add the reserved prawns with the chilli oil and coriander and cook for 1–2 minutes.

4 Stir in the lime juice and serve immediately.

Smoked Salmon Pâté

INGREDIENTS

450 g/1 lb smoked salmon, chopped into small pieces

1 tsp chopped fresh thyme

juice and finely grated zest of 1 small lemon

2 tbsp soft unsalted butter

85 g/3 oz soft cream cheese

pinch of paprika

pinch of cayenne pepper

pepper

crispbreads, to serve

makes about 450 g/1 lb

1 Put the smoked salmon, thyme, lemon juice and zest in a food processor or blender and process until just combined.

2 Scrape down the sides of the bowl and add the butter and cheese. Season lightly with the paprika, cayenne and pepper.

3 Process again until the mixture is blended, but not completely smooth – it should still have a slightly rough texture. Taste, and adjust the seasoning if necessary.

4 Transfer to an airtight container. Cover and leave to chill in the refrigerator until firm. Remove from the refrigerator at least 15 minutes before eating and serve with crispbreads.

Seared Salmon with Cannellini Bean Mash

INGREDIENTS

four x 175-g/6-oz salmon cutlets

finely grated zest and juice of 1 lemon

3 tbsp maple syrup

1 tbsp wholegrain mustard

½ tsp salt

FOR THE CANNELLINI BEAN MASH

three x 400-g/14-oz cans cannellini beans, drained

1 tbsp olive oil

5 tbsp crème fraîche

1 garlic clove, crushed

salt and pepper

serves ❹

1 Preheat the grill. Lay the salmon cutlets in a flameproof dish.

2 Mix the lemon zest and juice, maple syrup, mustard and ½ teaspoon of salt together in a bowl. Pour over the salmon and grill without turning for about 6 minutes until the salmon is cooked through.

3 For the mash, heat the beans, oil, crème fraîche and garlic in a saucepan until bubbling. Season with plenty of salt and pepper and mash with a wooden spoon.

4 Place the salmon alongside the mashed beans and pour over the cooking juices.

Peppered Tuna Steaks

INGREDIENTS

four x 175-g/6-oz tuna steaks

4 tsp sunflower or olive oil

1 tsp salt

2 tbsp pink, green and black
peppercorns, coarsely crushed

TO SERVE

4 baked potatoes (optional)

2 tbsp butter (optional)

handful of fresh rocket leaves

lemon wedges

serves ❹

1 Brush the tuna steaks with the oil and
sprinkle with salt.

2 Coat the tuna in the crushed peppercorns.

3 Meanwhile, heat a ridged griddle pan or
frying pan and, when hot, add the fish and
cook over a medium heat for 2–3 minutes on
each side. Serve with baked potatoes, if
desired, dabbed with a little butter, some
rocket leaves and the lemon wedges on
the side.

Fish Goujons with Chilli Mayonnaise

INGREDIENTS

200 g/7 oz plain flour

salt and pepper

3 eggs

140 g/5 oz matzo meal

450 g/1 lb firm white fish, such as monkfish, cut into strips

sunflower or groundnut oil, for frying

FOR THE CHILLI MAYONNAISE

2 tbsp sweet chilli sauce

4–5 tbsp mayonnaise

serves ❹

1 Mix the flour with plenty of salt and pepper on a large flat plate. Beat the eggs in a bowl and spread the matzo meal out on another flat plate.

2 Dip the fish pieces into the seasoned flour, then into the beaten egg, then into the matzo meal, ensuring a generous coating.

3 Pour the oil into a non-stick or heavy-based frying pan to give a depth of 1 cm/½ inch, then heat it up. Cook the fish pieces in batches for a few minutes, turning once, until golden and cooked through.

4 To make the chilli mayonnaise, beat the chilli sauce and mayonnaise together in a bowl until combined.

5 Transfer the fish to warmed plates and serve with the chilli mayonnaise on the side.

Lemon & Parsley Crusted Monkfish

INGREDIENTS

4 tbsp sunflower oil
or melted butter

4 tbsp fresh breadcrumbs

4 tbsp chopped fresh parsley

finely grated zest of 1 large
lemon

4 monkfish fillets, about
140–175 g/5–6 oz

salt and pepper

fresh sprigs of parsley,
to garnish

4 potatoes, peeled, cubed
and deep-fried, to serve
(optional)

serves ❹

1 Preheat the oven to 180°C/350°F/Gas Mark 4.
Mix the oil, breadcrumbs, parsley and lemon
zest with a sprinkling of salt and pepper
together in a bowl to give a smooth mixture.

2 Place the fish fillets on a large roasting tray.
Divide the breadcrumb mixture between them
and press it down onto the fish with your fingers
to ensure it covers the fillets.

3 Bake in the oven for 7–8 minutes or until
the fish is cooked. Garnish with fresh sprigs
of parsley, and serve with deep-fried potato
cubes, if desired.

Seafood Kebabs

INGREDIENTS

450 g/1 lb skinless, boneless fish, such as monkfish, swordfish and halibut

1 lemon, cut into 8 wedges

8 bay leaves

3 tbsp olive oil

serves ❷ to ❹

1 Preheat the grill. Cut the fish into cubes and thread onto 4 pre-soaked, wooden skewers alternately with the lemon and bay leaves.

2 Brush with oil and cook under a medium-hot grill for about 4 minutes on each side until the fish is cooked. Serve.

Microwave Herbed Fish Parcels

INGREDIENTS

four x 115 g/4 oz firm white fish fillets, such as monkfish

4 tbsp lemon juice

4 tbsp cider or white wine

4 tbsp chopped fresh parsley

4 fresh thyme sprigs

4 fresh rosemary sprigs

4 tomatoes, thinly sliced

serves ❹

1 Place a fish fillet in the centre of four x 30-cm/12-inch squares of baking paper.

2 Sprinkle each fillet with 1 tablespoon of lemon juice and 1 tablespoon of cider, followed by 1 tablespoon of chopped parsley. Add a sprig of thyme and rosemary to each parcel.

3 Arrange the sliced tomatoes over each fillet, overlapping them. Fold in the edges of the baking paper squares to completely enclose the filling and form parcels. Place the parcels in a circle on a heatproof plate, leaving a 2.5-cm/1-inch space between each parcel, and cook in the microwave oven on HIGH for 7 minutes. Serve immediately.

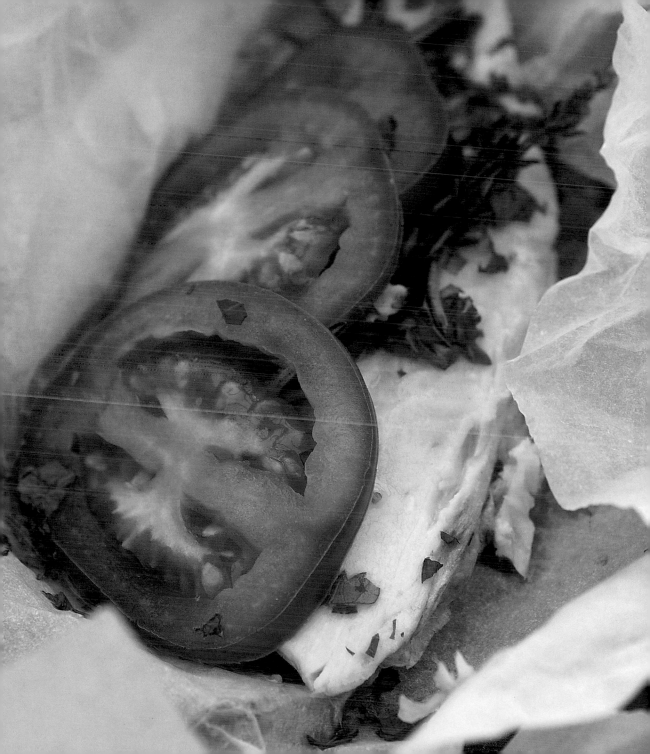

Spicy Tuna Fishcakes

INGREDIENTS

4 tbsp plain flour

salt and pepper

200 g/7 oz canned tuna in oil, drained

2–3 tbsp curry paste

1 spring onion, trimmed and finely chopped

1 egg, beaten

sunflower or groundnut oil, for frying

rocket leaves, to serve

makes ❹ fishcakes

1 Mix the flour with plenty of salt and pepper on a large flat plate. Mash the tuna with the curry paste, spring onion and beaten egg in a large bowl.

2 Form into 4 patties and dust in the seasoned flour.

3 Heat the oil in a frying pan, add the patties and fry for 3–4 minutes on each side until crisp and golden. Serve on a bed of rocket leaves.

4 Egg and Cheese

Eggs must be the original fast food because they take just minutes to cook. Cheese adds flavour and texture to all sorts of dishes, and you can change the flavour of any of these recipes by using different varieties of cheese. Always keep some eggs and cheese in the refrigerator and you'll never be stuck for a tasty meal!

Spiced Scrambled Eggs

INGREDIENTS

4 eggs

150 ml/5 fl oz single cream

salt and pepper

pinch of saffron

25 g/1 oz butter

½ tsp ground cumin

½–1 tsp harissa paste

1 tsp ground coriander

TO SERVE

2 pieces of freshly toasted
bread, buttered if desired

serves ❷

1 Whisk the eggs, cream, salt and pepper and saffron together in a bowl.

2 Melt the butter in a frying pan and add the cumin, harissa and ground coriander. Cook gently for 1 minute.

3 Pour in the egg mixture and cook, stirring, for a few minutes until the eggs are just set. Serve the spiced scrambled eggs on top of the freshly toasted bread.

Provençal Frittata

INGREDIENTS

3 tbsp sunflower or olive oil

1 garlic clove, chopped

225 g/8 oz fresh or frozen spinach

salt and pepper

handful of cherry tomatoes, halved

6 eggs, whisked

cherry tomatoes on the vine, to serve (optional)

serves ❷ to ❹

1 Heat the oil in a large frying pan, add the garlic and cook for 1 minute then add the spinach and cook for a further 1 minute until wilted.

2 Season with salt and pepper, add the cherry tomatoes to the pan and cook for 1 minute.

3 Pour the eggs into the frying pan, stirring, and cook for 4–5 minutes until set. Serve hot or cold cut into wedges, with cherry tomatoes on the vine, if desired.

Egg & Bacon Salad

INGREDIENTS

1 tbsp sunflower or olive oil

6–8 slices streaky bacon, diced

55 g/2 oz fresh breadcrumbs

selection of salad leaves, torn

6–8 hard-boiled eggs, quartered

12 black olives

2 tbsp white wine vinegar

5 tbsp extra virgin olive oil

1 tbsp wholegrain mustard

salt and pepper

serves ❹

1 Heat the sunflower or olive oil in a frying pan, add the bacon and cook for about 5 minutes until crisp. Remove from the pan.

2 Add the breadcrumbs to the pan and cook over a high heat until crisp and golden. Set aside.

3 Put the salad leaves into a bowl with the eggs and olives and tip in the bacon.

4 Whisk the vinegar, extra virgin olive oil, mustard and salt and pepper together in a bowl and pour over the salad.

5 Toss to mix, sprinkle with the crisp breadcrumbs and serve immediately.

Spaghetti Carbonara

INGREDIENTS

450 g/1 lb fresh spaghetti

25 g/1 oz butter

6 slices streaky bacon, diced

3 eggs

2 tbsp single cream

4 tbsp freshly grated
Parmesan cheese

salt and pepper

chopped fresh parsley,
for sprinkling

serves ❹

1 Cook the spaghetti in a large saucepan of boiling salted water for about 2–4 minutes, or according to the packet instructions, until tender but still firm to the bite.

2 Meanwhile, heat the butter in a frying pan, add the bacon and cook until crisp. Keep warm.

3 Beat the eggs, cream, cheese, and salt and pepper together in a bowl.

4 As soon as the spaghetti is cooked, drain and return to the pan over a low heat.

5 Add the bacon, and egg and cream mixture, and quickly toss the spaghetti several times until the sauce begins to thicken and the spaghetti is coated. Serve immediately sprinkled with chopped parsley.

Goat's Cheese Tarts

INGREDIENTS

butter, for greasing

400 g/14 oz packet ready-rolled puff pastry

1 tbsp plain flour

1 egg, beaten

3 tbsp onion or tomato relish

three x 115-g/4-oz goat's cheese logs, sliced

olive oil, for drizzling

pepper

makes about ⑫ tarts

1 Preheat the oven to 200°C/400°F/Gas Mark 6 and grease several baking trays.

2 Cut out as many 7.5-cm/3-inch rounds as possible from the pastry on a lightly floured work surface.

3 Place the rounds on the baking trays and press gently about 2.5 cm/1 inch from the edge of each with a smaller 5-cm/2-inch pastry cutter.

4 Brush the rounds with beaten egg and prick with a fork.

5 Top each circle with a little relish and a slice of goat's cheese. Drizzle with oil and sprinkle over a little black pepper.

6 Bake for 8–10 minutes, or until the pastry is crisp and the cheese is bubbling. Serve warm.

Warm Goat's Cheese Salad

INGREDIENTS

1 small iceberg lettuce, torn into pieces

handful of rocket leaves

few radicchio leaves, torn

6 slices French bread

115 g/4 oz goat's cheese, sliced

FOR THE DRESSING

4 tbsp extra virgin olive oil

1 tbsp white wine vinegar

salt and pepper

serves ❹

1 Preheat the grill. Divide all the leaves between 4 individual salad bowls.

2 Toast one side of the bread under the grill until golden. Place a slice of cheese on top of each untoasted side and toast until the cheese is just melting.

3 Put all the dressing ingredients into a bowl and beat together until combined. Pour over the leaves, tossing to coat.

4 Cut each slice of bread in half and place 3 halves on top of each salad. Toss very gently to combine and serve warm.

Pizza Express

INGREDIENTS

23-cm/9-inch ready-made thin-crust pizza base or 1 ciabatta loaf, sliced horizontally

fresh basil leaves, torn

FOR THE TOMATO TOPPING

150 ml/5 fl oz tomato passata

3 tbsp tomato purée

2 garlic cloves, crushed

pinch each of sugar, salt and pepper

handful of cherry tomatoes

FOR THE CHEESE TOPPING

150 ml/5 fl oz tomato passata

3 tbsp tomato purée

115 g/4 oz jar roasted peppers, drained and thickly sliced

a few black olives

115 g/4 oz firm mozzarella cheese, grated

55 g/2 oz Parmesan cheese, grated

salt and pepper

serves 4 to 6

1 Preheat the oven to 200°C/400°F/Gas Mark 6. To make the tomato topping, mix the passata, tomato purée, garlic, sugar and salt and pepper together in a bowl. Spread over the ready-made pizza base and scatter with the cherry tomatoes.

2 To make the cheese topping, mix the tomato passata and tomato purée together in a bowl and spread over the pizza base. Top with the peppers and the olives. Season with salt and pepper and scatter the mozzarella and Parmesan cheeses over the top.

3 Bake in the oven for 8–10 minutes until hot and bubbling. Scatter with basil leaves and serve immediately.

Creamy Ricotta, Mint & Garlic Pasta

INGREDIENTS

300 g/10½ oz short fresh pasta shapes

salt and pepper

140 g/5 oz ricotta cheese

1–2 roasted garlic cloves from a jar, finely chopped

150 ml/5 fl oz double cream

1 tbsp chopped fresh mint and 4 sprigs, to garnish

serves ❹

1 Cook the pasta in a large saucepan of boiling salted water for about 3 minutes, or according to the packet instructions until tender but still firm to the bite.

2 Beat the ricotta, garlic, cream and chopped mint together in a bowl until smooth.

3 Drain the cooked pasta then tip back into the pan. Pour in the cheese mixture and toss together.

4 Season with pepper and serve immediately, garnished with the sprigs of mint.

Baked Chilli Cheese Sandwiches

INGREDIENTS

350 g/12 oz grated cheese, such as Cheddar

115 g/4 oz butter, softened, plus extra to finish

4 fresh green chillies, deseeded and chopped

½ tsp ground cumin

8 thick slices bread

makes 4 sandwiches

1 Preheat the oven to 190°C/375°F/Gas Mark 5. Mix the cheese and butter together in a bowl until creamy then add the chillies and cumin.

2 Spread this mixture over 4 slices of bread and top with the remaining slices.

3 Spread the outside of the sandwiches with extra butter and bake for 8–10 minutes until crisp. Serve.

Caramel-topped Brie

INGREDIENTS

2 tbsp water

175 g/6 oz granulated sugar

1 whole mini Brie cheese

TO SERVE (OPTIONAL)

8 oatcakes

4 handfuls fresh, washed
white grapes

serves **4**

1 Heat the water and sugar in a saucepan over a low heat until the sugar has dissolved completely.

2 Increase the heat and cook steadily until the sugar is a dark golden colour.

3 Remove the pan from the heat then immediately pour over the Brie and leave to set. Serve at room temperature: crack the caramel before serving, with oatcakes and fresh grapes, if desired.

Grilled Halloumi
with Herbed Couscous

INGREDIENTS

450 g/1 lb halloumi cheese,
cut into 5-mm/¼-inch slices

4 tbsp chilli oil

FOR THE HERBED COUSCOUS

400 ml/14 fl oz hot vegetable
stock

225 g/8 oz couscous

2 tbsp chopped fresh mixed
herbs

2 tsp lemon juice

1 tbsp olive oil

serves ❹

1 Preheat the grill to high and line the grill
rack with foil.

2 Put the cheese slices in a bowl, pour over
the chilli oil and toss well to coat the cheese.

3 Place the cheese on the grill rack and cook
under the grill for 2–3 minutes on each side
until golden.

4 Meanwhile, stir the hot stock into the
couscous in a large bowl. Cover and leave
to stand for 5 minutes.

5 Stir the herbs, lemon juice and olive oil
into the couscous. Serve with the grilled
halloumi cheese.

Mozzarella Gnocchi

INGREDIENTS

butter, for greasing

450 g/1 lb packet potato gnocchi

200 ml/7 fl oz double cream

225 g/8 oz firm mozzarella cheese, grated or chopped

salt and pepper

serves ❷ to ❹

1 Preheat the grill and grease a large baking dish.

2 Cook the gnocchi in a large saucepan of boiling salted water for about 3 minutes, or according to the packet instructions.

3 Drain and put into the prepared baking dish.

4 Season the cream with salt and pepper and drizzle over the gnocchi. Scatter over the cheese and cook under the grill for a few minutes until the top is browned and bubbling. Serve immediately.

5 Vegetarian

Colourful tasty vegetables with clear well-defined flavours are delicious in their own right. Ringing the changes by adding different herbs to recipes, such as a sprinkling of chopped mint to a pea soup recipe, will completely alter the flavour. A handful of chopped toasted nuts or crumbled cheese will also add interest and colour to plain salads.

Chilled Avocado Soup

INGREDIENTS

4 ripe avocados, peeled

1 garlic clove

1.2 litres/2 pints vegetable stock

4 tbsp lime juice

pinch of cayenne pepper

salt and pepper

2 tbsp chives, snipped, to garnish

French bread, to serve

serves **6**

1 Put the avocados, garlic, stock, lime juice and cayenne into a food processor or blender and process until smooth.

2 Season with salt and pepper to taste and leave to chill in the refrigerator until ready to serve with French bread and garnished with snipped chives.

Garden Pea Soup

INGREDIENTS

600 ml/1 pint vegetable stock

450 g/1 lb fresh peas

pinch of granulated sugar

salt and pepper

125 ml/4 fl oz single cream

TO SERVE

2 tbsp single cream

4 crusty rolls

serves ❹

1 Bring the stock to the boil in a large saucepan. Add the peas and cook for 5 minutes.

2 Remove the pan from the heat, season with sugar, and salt and pepper, then transfer to a food processor or blender and process until smooth.

3 Pour into a saucepan, stir in the cream and heat gently to simmering point.

4 Taste and adjust the seasoning if necessary, then pour into 4 serving bowls, adding a swirl of single cream to each bowl and serving with crusty rolls.

Quesadillas

INGREDIENTS

4 tbsp finely chopped fresh
jalapeño chillies

1 onion, chopped

1 tbsp red wine vinegar

5 tbsp extra virgin olive oil

300–400 g/10½–14 oz canned
sweetcorn

8 soft flour tortillas

serves ❹

1 Put the chillies, onion, vinegar and 4
tablespoons of olive oil in a food processor
or blender and process until finely chopped.

2 Tip into a bowl and stir in the sweetcorn.

3 Heat the remaining oil in a frying pan, add
a tortilla and cook for 1 minute until golden.

4 Spread the chilli mixture over the tortilla
and fold over.

5 Cook for 2–3 minutes until golden and the
filling is heated through. Remove from the pan
and keep warm. Repeat with the other tortillas
and filling. Serve immediately.

Creamed Mushrooms

INGREDIENTS

juice of 1 small lemon

450 g/1 lb small button mushrooms

25 g/1oz butter

1 tbsp sunflower or olive oil

1 small onion, finely chopped

125 ml/4 fl oz whipping or double cream

salt and pepper

1 tbsp chopped fresh parsley, plus 4 sprigs, to garnish

serves 4

1 Sprinkle a little of the lemon juice over the mushrooms.

2 Heat the butter and oil in a frying pan, add the onion and cook for 1 minute. Add the mushrooms, shaking the pan so they do not stick.

3 Season to taste with salt and pepper, then stir in the cream, chopped parsley and remaining lemon juice.

4 Heat until hot but do not allow to boil then transfer to a serving plate and garnish with the parsley sprigs. Serve immediately.

Tofu Stir-fry

INGREDIENTS

2 tbsp sunflower or olive oil

350 g/12 oz firm tofu, cubed

225 g/8 oz pak choi, roughly chopped

1 garlic clove, chopped

4 tbsp sweet chilli sauce

2 tbsp light soy sauce

serves ❹

1 Heat 1 tablespoon of oil in a wok, add the tofu in batches and stir-fry for 2–3 minutes until golden. Remove and set aside.

2 Add the pak choi to the wok and stir-fry for a few seconds until tender and wilted. Remove and set aside.

3 Add the remaining oil to the wok, then add the garlic and stir-fry for 30 seconds.

4 Stir in the chilli sauce and soy sauce and bring to the boil.

5 Return the tofu and pak choi to the wok and toss gently until coated in the sauce. Serve immediately.

Noodle Stir-fry

INGREDIENTS

140 g/5 oz flat rice noodles

6 tbsp soy sauce

2 tbsp lemon juice

1 tsp granulated sugar

½ tsp cornflour

1 tbsp vegetable oil

2 tsp grated fresh root ginger

2 garlic cloves, chopped

4–5 spring onions, trimmed and sliced

2 tbsp rice wine or dry sherry

200 g/7 oz canned water chestnuts, sliced

serves ❷

1 Put the noodles in a large bowl and cover with boiling water. Leave to stand for 4 minutes. Drain and rinse under cold running water.

2 Mix the soy sauce, lemon juice, sugar and cornflour together in small bowl.

3 Heat the oil in a wok, add the ginger and garlic and stir-fry for 1 minute.

4 Add the spring onions and stir-fry for 3 minutes.

5 Add the rice wine or dry sherry, followed by the soy sauce mixture and cook for 1 minute.

6 Stir in the water chestnuts and noodles and cook for a further 1–2 minutes, or until heated through. Serve immediately.

Falafel Burgers

INGREDIENTS

two x 400-g/14-oz cans chickpeas, drained and rinsed

1 small onion, chopped

zest and juice of 1 lime

2 tsp ground coriander

2 tsp ground cumin

6 tbsp plain flour

4 tbsp olive oil

4 sprigs fresh basil, to garnish

tomato salsa, to serve

serves ❹

1 Put the chickpeas, onion, lime zest and juice and the spices into a food processor and process to a coarse paste.

2 Tip the mixture out onto a clean work surface or chopping board and shape into 4 patties.

3 Spread the flour out on a large flat plate and use to coat the patties.

4 Heat the oil in a large frying pan, add the burgers and cook for 2 minutes on each side until crisp. Garnish with basil and serve with tomato salsa.

Tagliatelle with Lemon & Thyme

INGREDIENTS

350 g/12 oz fresh tagliatelle

85g/3 oz butter

finely grated zest and juice
of 1 lemon

2 tbsp chopped fresh thyme

salt and pepper

serves ❷ to ❹

1 Cook the pasta in a large saucepan of boiling salted water for about 4 minutes, or according to the packet instructions until tender but still firm to the bite.

2 Drain the pasta, keeping about 3 tablespoons of the cooking liquid in it. Stir in the butter, grated lemon zest and lemon juice, thyme, and salt and pepper, and toss well to mix. Serve immediately.

Pasta with Spicy Olive Sauce

INGREDIENTS

350 g/12 oz fresh pasta shapes

salt, plus extra for cooking
the pasta

6 tbsp olive oil

½ tsp freshly grated nutmeg

½ tsp black pepper

1 garlic clove, crushed

2 tbsp tapenade

85g/3 oz black or green olives,
stoned and sliced

1 tbsp chopped fresh parsley,
to garnish (optional)

serves ❷ to ❹

1 Cook the pasta in a large saucepan of boiling salted water for about 4 minutes, or according to the packet instructions until tender but still firm to the bite.

2 Meanwhile, put ½ teaspoon of salt with the oil, nutmeg, pepper, garlic, tapenade and olives in another saucepan and heat slowly but don't allow to boil. Cover and leave to stand for 3–4 minutes.

3 Drain the pasta and return to the saucepan. Add the flavoured oil and heat gently for 1–2 minutes. Serve immediately garnished, with chopped parsley, if using.

Chinese-style Gingered Vegetables

INGREDIENTS

1 tbsp sunflower or
groundnut oil

2.5-cm/1-inch piece fresh root
ginger, peeled and grated

1 onion, thinly sliced

115 g/4 oz frozen French
beans, cut into small pieces

450 g/1 lb bag frozen mixed
vegetables

150 ml/5 fl oz water

2 heaped tbsp dark brown
sugar

2 tbsp cornflour

4 tbsp malt vinegar

4 tbsp soy sauce

1 tsp ground ginger

serves ❷

1 Heat the oil in a wok or large frying pan, add the grated ginger and fry for 1 minute. Remove from the wok or pan and drain on kitchen paper.

2 Reduce the heat slightly and add the vegetables and water to the wok.

3 Cover with a lid or foil and cook for 5–6 minutes, or until the vegetables are tender.

4 Mix the sugar, cornflour, malt vinegar, soy sauce and ground ginger together in a bowl. Increase the heat to medium and add the mixture to the vegetables in the wok. Simmer for 1 minute, stirring, until thickened.

5 Return the ginger to the wok and stir to mix well. Heat through for 2 minutes and then serve immediately.

Vegetable Tartlets

INGREDIENTS

butter, for greasing

12 ready-baked puff pastry cases

2 tbsp olive oil

1 red pepper, deseeded and diced

1 garlic clove, crushed

1 small onion, finely chopped

225 g/8 oz ripe tomatoes, chopped

1 tbsp torn fresh basil

1 tsp fresh or dried thyme

salt and pepper

green salad, to serve

makes 12 tartlets

1 Preheat the oven to 200°C/400°F/Gas Mark 6 and grease several baking trays.

2 Place the ready-baked pastry cases on the prepared baking trays.

3 Heat the oil in a frying pan, add the pepper, garlic and onion and cook over a high heat for about 3 minutes until soft.

4 Add the tomatoes, herbs and seasoning and spoon onto the pastry cases.

5 Bake for about 5 minutes, or until the filling is piping hot. Serve warm with a green salad.

Wilted Spinach, Yogurt & Walnut Salad

INGREDIENTS

450 g/1 lb fresh spinach leaves

1 onion, chopped

1 tbsp olive oil

salt and pepper

225 ml/8 fl oz natural yogurt

1 garlic clove, finely chopped

2 tbsp chopped toasted walnuts

2–3 tsp chopped fresh mint

pitta bread, to serve

serves 2

1 Put the spinach and onion into a saucepan, cover and cook gently for a few minutes until the spinach has wilted.

2 Add the oil and cook for a further 5 minutes. Season to taste with salt and pepper.

3 Combine the yogurt and garlic in a bowl.

4 Put the spinach and onion into a serving bowl and pour over the yogurt mixture. Scatter over the walnuts and chopped mint and serve with pitta bread.

Moroccan Carrot & Orange Salad

INGREDIENTS

450 g/1 lb carrots, peeled

1 tbsp olive oil

2 tbsp lemon juice

pinch of granulated sugar

2 large oranges, peeled and cut into segments (any juices reserved)

55 g/2 oz raisins

1 tsp ground cinnamon

2 tbsp toasted pine kernels

serves ❹

1 Grate the carrots into a large bowl.

2 In a separate bowl, combine the oil, lemon juice, sugar, and orange juice from the orange segments.

3 Toss the orange segments with the carrots and stir in the raisins and cinnamon.

4 Pour over the dressing and scatter over the pine kernels just before serving.

Hot Tomato & Basil Salad

INGREDIENTS

700 g/1 lb 9 oz cherry tomatoes

1 garlic clove, crushed

2 tbsp capers, drained and rinsed

1 tsp granulated sugar

4 tbsp olive oil

2 tbsp torn fresh basil

serves ❻

1 Preheat the oven to 200°C/400°F/Gas Mark 6. Stir the tomatoes, garlic, capers and sugar together in a bowl and tip into a roasting tin.

2 Pour over the oil and toss to coat.

3 Cook in the oven for 10 minutes until the tomatoes are hot.

4 Remove from the oven and tip into a heatproof serving bowl. Scatter over the basil and serve immediately.

6 Fruit

Fresh fruit is one of the healthiest and most delicious ways to end a meal. Make an unusual fruit salad with a variety of seasonal fruits steeped in lemonade or ginger beer. A quick snack that children love is bananas coated in melted chocolate (milk, plain or white) and rolled in desiccated coconut or chopped nuts.

Pan-fried Apples or Pears
with Maple Syrup & Walnuts

INGREDIENTS

85 g/3 oz butter

4 firm apples or pears,
cut into thick slices

3 tbsp maple syrup

2 tbsp brandy

4 tbsp walnuts

serves ❹

1 Melt half the butter in a frying pan and add half the apples or pears.

2 Cook for 2 minutes on each side until golden. Remove from the pan and cook the remaining fruit, then remove from the pan.

3 Add the remaining butter to the frying pan with the maple syrup, brandy and walnuts and bring to the boil. Remove from the heat.

4 Put the warm fruit into serving bowls and pour over the sauce. Serve.

Strawberry & Banana Cream

INGREDIENTS

4 large bananas

450 g/1 lb strawberries, hulled, plus extra whole strawberries to decorate

300 ml/10 fl oz double cream, whipped

granulated or caster sugar, if necessary

biscuits, to serve

serves ❹ to ❻

1 Peel the bananas and put in a food processor with the strawberries. Process to a purée and tip into a large bowl.

2 Gently stir in the whipped cream. Sweeten to taste if needed.

3 Chill in the refrigerator until you are ready to serve. Serve decorated with a whole strawberry and biscuits.

Berry Brûlées

INGREDIENTS

450 g/1 lb berries, such as raspberries, strawberries, redcurrants and stoned cherries

300 ml/10 fl oz double cream

115 g/4 oz caster sugar

serves 4 to 6

1 Preheat the grill to very hot. Divide the berries into 4–6 individual flameproof dishes or one large dish.

2 Whip the cream in a large bowl until thick but not stiff.

3 Spoon the cream over the berries until they are evenly covered.

4 Sprinkle over the sugar to cover the cream completely and place under the grill, about 5–7.5 cm/2–3 inches from the heat source, for about 3 minutes, or until the sugar is bubbling and golden. Watch the sugar carefully – it will scorch if left too long.

Little Lemon Pots

INGREDIENTS

150 ml/5 fl oz double cream

200 ml/7 fl oz condensed milk

grated zest and juice of 2 lemons

amaretti biscuits, to serve (optional)

serves ❹ to ❻

1 Mix the cream and condensed milk together in a bowl until thoroughly combined.

2 Stir in the lemon zest and juice.

3 Pour into 4–6 serving dishes and leave to chill in the refrigerator until ready to serve. Serve with amaretti biscuits, if using.

Caramelized Pineapple Slices

INGREDIENTS

6 thick slices pineapple

juice of 1 large orange

6 tbsp light brown sugar

makes 6 slices

1 Preheat the grill. Lay the pineapple slices on a baking tray or on a grill pan and sprinkle with half the orange juice.

2 Sprinkle with half the sugar and grill for 2–3 minutes until the sugar is bubbling and caramelized.

3 Turn the slices over and sprinkle with the remaining orange juice and sugar. Grill for another 2–3 minutes and serve.

Plums in Spiced Red Wine

INGREDIENTS

300 ml/10 fl oz red wine

3 heaped tbsp dark brown sugar

1 cinnamon stick, broken

4 cardamom pods, cracked

pinch of ground cloves

8 firm red plums, stoned and halved

4 tbsp crème fraîche, to serve (optional)

serves ❷ to ❹

1 Put the red wine, sugar, cinnamon, cardamom and ground cloves in a saucepan and slowly bring to the boil, stirring until the sugar has dissolved completely.

2 Add the plums to the saucepan and cook gently for about 5 minutes.

3 Remove from the heat and leave to cool completely before serving with crème fraîche, if desired.

Grilled Tropical Fruits with Spiced Butter

INGREDIENTS

115 g/4 oz unsalted butter

2 tbsp stem ginger, chopped

½ tsp ground cinnamon

½ tsp grated nutmeg

2 tsp lemon juice

2 tsp icing sugar

4 halved bananas

4 pineapple wedges

2 pawpaws, sliced

1 mango, sliced

serves ❹

1 Preheat the grill or barbecue. Cream the butter with the spices, lemon juice and icing sugar in a large bowl.

2 Spread half of the spicy butter mixture over the pieces of fruit.

3 Place the fruit on the grill rack and grill for 2–3 minutes until beginning to caramelize.

4 Turn the fruit over and repeat with the remaining mixture. Serve.

Cherry Mascarpone Creams

INGREDIENTS

425 g/15 oz canned black cherries in syrup, stoned

1 tbsp rosewater

500 g/1 lb 2 oz mascarpone cheese

flaked toasted almonds or chopped pistachio nuts, to decorate

serves ❹

1 Drain the cherries and reserve 2 tablespoons of the syrup.

2 Stir the rosewater into the reserved cherry syrup, then stir in the cherries.

3 Spoon into 4 serving dishes. Cover with the mascarpone and sprinkle with the almonds or pistachios. Leave to chill in the refrigerator until ready to serve.

Orange & Caramel Bananas

INGREDIENTS

115 g/4 oz granulated
or caster sugar

1 tsp vanilla extract

finely grated zest and
juice of 1 orange

4 bananas, peeled
and thickly sliced

2 tbsp butter

serves ❹

1 Put the sugar, vanilla extract and orange juice in a frying pan and heat gently until it forms a caramel.

2 Add the banana slices and cook, shaking the pan, for 1–2 minutes until they are coated with the caramel.

3 Add the butter to the pan and cook for a further 3 minutes shaking the pan to coat the bananas.

4 Tip the bananas onto a serving plate and sprinkle with the orange zest. Serve.

7 Desserts

Finishing touches make a huge difference to the appearance of desserts. Crushed biscuits, finely grated citrus zest, or chocolate curls make impressive decorations. To make chocolate curls, use a vegetable peeler to shave off long pieces from a chocolate bar. A quick dusting of icing sugar sifted over desserts just before serving also adds a stylish finish.

Brown Sugar Mocha Cream Dessert

INGREDIENTS

300 ml/10 fl oz double cream

1 tsp vanilla extract

85 g/3 oz fresh wholemeal breadcrumbs

85 g/3 oz dark brown sugar

1 tbsp instant coffee granules

2 tbsp cocoa powder

grated chocolate, to decorate (optional)

serves ❹ to ❻

1 Whip the cream and vanilla extract together in a large bowl until thick and softly peaking.

2 Mix the breadcrumbs, sugar, coffee and cocoa powder together in another large bowl and layer the dry mixture with the whipped cream in serving glasses, ending with whipped cream. Sprinkle with grated chocolate, if using.

3 Cover tightly and leave to chill in the refrigerator for several hours, or overnight.

Ginger Baked Alaskas

INGREDIENTS

4 tbsp sultanas or raisins

3 tbsp dark rum or ginger wine

4 square slices ginger cake

4 scoops vanilla ice cream or rum and raisin ice cream

3 egg whites

175 g/6 oz granulated or caster sugar

serves 4

1 Preheat the oven to 230°C/450°F/Gas Mark 8. Mix the sultanas with the rum in a small bowl.

2 Place the cake slices well apart on a baking sheet and scatter a spoonful of the soaked sultanas on each slice.

3 Place a scoop of ice cream in the centre of each slice and place in the freezer.

4 Meanwhile, whisk the egg whites in a large grease-free bowl until soft peaks form then gradually whisk the sugar into the egg whites, a tablespoonful at a time, until the mixture forms stiff peaks.

5 Remove the ice cream-topped cake slices from the freezer and spoon the meringue over the ice cream. Spread to cover the ice cream completely.

6 Bake in the oven for about 5 minutes until starting to brown. Serve immediately.

No-bake Chocolate Fudge Cake

INGREDIENTS

225 g/8 oz plain chocolate

225 g/8 oz unsalted butter

3 tbsp black coffee

55 g/2 oz light brown sugar

few drops of vanilla extract

225 g/8 oz digestive biscuits, crushed

85 g/3 oz raisins

85 g/3 oz walnuts, chopped

serves ❻ to ❽

1 Line a 450-g/1-lb loaf tin or a 20-cm/8-inch cake tin with greaseproof paper or non-stick baking paper. Melt the chocolate, butter, coffee, sugar and vanilla extract in a saucepan over a low heat.

2 Stir in the crushed biscuits and the raisins and walnuts and stir well.

3 Spoon the mixture into the prepared loaf tin.

4 Leave to set for 1–2 hours in the refrigerator, then turn out and cut into thin slices to serve.

White Wine & Honey Syllabub

INGREDIENTS

3 tbsp brandy

3 tbsp white wine

600 ml/1 pint double cream

6 tbsp clear honey

55 g/2 oz flaked almonds

serves ❹ to ❻

1 Combine the brandy and white wine in a bowl.

2 Whip the cream in a large bowl until just thickened.

3 Add the honey to the cream and whip again for about 15 seconds.

4 Pour the brandy and wine mixture in a continuous stream onto the cream and honey mixture, whisking constantly until all the liquid is absorbed and the mixture forms soft peaks.

5 Spoon into serving dishes and leave to chill in the refrigerator for 2–3 hours.

6 Just before serving scatter over the almonds.

Jamaican Cream

INGREDIENTS

300 ml/10 fl oz double cream

2 tbsp light brown sugar

1 tbsp strong coffee or coffee liqueur

2 tbsp dark rum

2 ripe bananas

chocolate-covered coffee beans, to decorate

serves ❷

1 Whip the cream, sugar and coffee together in a large bowl until thick and softly peaking.

2 Gradually fold in the rum.

3 Peel and slice the bananas, then gently stir into the mixture.

4 Spoon into serving glasses or bowls and top with chocolate-covered coffee beans. Leave to chill until ready to serve.

Cheat's Chocolate Pots

INGREDIENTS

140 g/5 oz good-quality plain chocolate, at least 60% cocoa solids, broken into small pieces or chopped

400 ml/14 fl oz double cream

1 tsp vanilla extract

serves 4 to 6

1 Melt the chocolate in a bowl set over a saucepan of simmering, not boiling, water, or melt in a glass or ceramic bowl in a microwave oven.

2 Remove the bowl from the pan or microwave and gradually stir in the cream and vanilla extract until the mixture is smooth.

3 Pour into small coffee cups or dishes and leave to chill in the refrigerator until ready to serve.

Mocha Creams

INGREDIENTS

12 marshmallows

125 ml/4 fl oz strong black coffee

55 g/2 oz plain chocolate, finely chopped or grated

300 ml/10 fl oz double cream

serves ❷ to ❹

1 Put the marshmallows in a saucepan with the coffee and half the chocolate. Heat gently until melted. Remove the pan from the heat.

2 Whip the cream in a large bowl until thick and softly peaking, then gently stir in the coffee mixture.

3 Spoon into 2–4 serving bowls or dishes and sprinkle with the remaining chocolate. Leave to chill in the refrigerator until ready to serve.

Index

Apple
  Pan-fried Apples with Maple
    Syrup & Walnuts 142
Avocado
  Chilled Avocado Soup 112

Bacon
  Egg & Bacon Salad 90
  Spaghetti Carbonara 92
Banana
  Orange & Caramel Bananas
    158
  Strawberry & Banana
    Cream 144
Beef
  Peppered Steaks in Whisky
    Cream Sauce 20
  Stir-fried Beef with Cashew
    Nuts 18
  Teriyaki Steak 14
  Vietnamese Beef Soup 16
Berries
  Berry Brûlées 146
  Strawberry & Banana
    Cream 144

Cheese
  Baked Chilli Cheese
    Sandwiches 102
  Caramel-topped Brie
    104
  Creamy Ricotta, Mint &
    Garlic Pasta 100
  Goat's Cheese Tarts 94
  Grilled Halloumi with
    Herbed Couscous 106
  Mozzarella Gnocchi 108
  Pizza Express 98
  Warm Goat's Cheese Salad
    96
Cherry
  Cherry Mascarpone Creams
    156
Chicken
  Chicken with Creamy Penne
    36
  Chicken in Marsala Sauce
    44
  Chicken Nuggets with
    Barbecue Sauce 42
  Chicken Satay 34

Fragrant Chicken 40
Stir-fried Coconut Chicken
  38

Desserts
  Brown Sugar Mocha Cream
    Dessert 162
  Cheat's Chocolate Pots 172
  Ginger Baked Alaskas 164
  Jamaican Cream 170
  Little Lemon Pots 148
  Mocha Creams 174
  No-bake Chocolate Fudge
    Cake 166
  White Wine & Honey
    Syllabub 168
Duck
  Asian Duck & Noodle Salad
    with Peanut Sauce 50
  Duck Breasts with Citrus
    Glaze 48
  Honeyed Duck Stir-fry 52

Eggs
  Egg & Bacon Salad 90
  Provençal Frittata 88
  Spaghetti Carbonara 92
  Spiced Scambled Eggs 86

Falafel
  Falafel Burgers 124
Fish
  Fish Goujons with Chilli
    Mayonnaise 74
  Lemon & Parsley Crusted
    Monkfish 76
  Microwave Herbed Fish
    Parcels 80
  Peppered Tuna Steaks 72
  Seared Salmon with
    Cannellini Bean Mash 70
  Smoked Salmon Pâté 68
  Spicy Tuna Fishcakes 82

Ham
  Florentine Ham 28
  Pancetta-wrapped Scallops
    62
  Turkey Cutlets with Parma
    Ham & Sage 46

Lamb
  Herbed Lamb Burgers 12
  Orange & Lemon-coated
    Crispy Lamb Cutlets 10

Mushroom
  Creamed Mushrooms 118

Pasta
  Chicken with Creamy Penne
    36
  Creamy Ricotta, Mint &
    Garlic Pasta 100
  Pasta with Spicy Olive
    Sauce 128
  Spaghetti Carbonara 92
  Tagliatelle with Lemon &
    Thyme 126
Pea
  Garden Pea Soup 114
Pear
  Pan-fried Pears with Maple
    Syrup & Walnuts 142
Pineapple
  Caramelized Pineapple
    Slices 150
Plum
  Plums in Spiced Red Wine
    152
Pork
  Ginger Pork 24
  Spicy Pork Meatballs 22
  Sweet & Sour Pork 26

Salad
  Asian Duck & Noodle Salad
    with Peanut Sauce 50
  Egg & Bacon Salad 90
  Hot Tomato & Basil Salad
    138
  Moroccan Carrot & Orange
    Salad 136
  Warm Goat's Cheese Salad
    96
  Wilted Spinach, Yogurt &
    Walnut Salad 134
Seafood
  Garlic-sizzled Prawns with
    Chilli Dipping Sauce 56
  Hot & Sour Prawn Soup 66
  Oysters au Gratin 60

Pancetta-wrapped Scallops
  62
Poached Scallops with
  Sweet Dill Dressing 64
Seafood Kebabs 78
Wine-steamed Mussels 58
Soup
  Chilled Avocado Soup 112
  Garden Pea Soup 114
  Hot & Sour Prawn Soup 66
  Vietnamese Beef Soup 16
Spinach
  Wilted Spinach, Yogurt &
    Walnut Salad 134
Stir-fry
  Chinese-style Gingered
    Vegetables 130
  Honeyed Duck Stir-fry 52
  Noodle Stir-fry 122
  Stir-fried Beef with Cashew
    Nuts 18
  Stir-fried Coconut Chicken
    38
  Tofu Stir-fry 120

Tarts
  Goat's Cheese Tarts 94
  Vegetable Tartlets 132
Tofu
  Tofu Stir-fry 120
Tortilla
  Quesadillas 116
Tropical fruit
  Grilled Tropical Fruits with
    Spiced Butter 154
Turkey
  Turkey Cutlets with Parma
    Ham & Sage 46

Venison
  Venison Steaks in
    Redcurrant Cream Sauce
    30